MW00565544

The Time It Takes Light

For David and Sally Stratman,
over whose table many of
these were first voiced
Love,
Dick

The Time It Takes Light

Richard Hague (signature)

Poems by Richard Hague

Word Press

© 2004 by Richard Hague

Published by Word Press
P.O. Box 541106
Cincinnati, OH 45254-1106

ISBN: 0-9717371-9-3
LCCN: 2003104793

Poetry Editor: Kevin Walzer
Business Editor: Lori Jareo

Typeset in Garamond by WordTech Communications, Cincinnati, OH

Visit us on the web at www.word-press.com

Acknowledgments

Grateful acknowledgement is made to the following journals in which many of the poems in this book have appeared:

Asheville Poetry Review: "Picasso Writes to Niels Bohr at Los Alamos" and "The Sky Is Falling. Do You Really Want to Be Writing?"

Birmingham Poetry Review: "Up by its Bootstraps, or Tongue of Chameleon as a Slice of Field," "The Poetry of Heat," "Light," and "Brief Test in Physics"

Nimrod: International Journal of Prose and Poetry: "In a Collective Nightmare, Mr. M. Instructs the Whole Class," "Mr. M. Accelerates," "Mr. M. and Mr. H. Talk over Lunch," "Rejecting the Sargent-Welch Scientific Company's Measuring Kit in Mr. M.'s Physics Lab," and "Essay of the Body as Cloud Chamber"

Writing Across the Curriculum notes: "Box Marked 'Hazardous Materials'…"

Sarasota Poetry Theater, "Soulspeak" First Prize: "Cosmology: The Word on the Street"

Sow's Ear Poetry Review: "The Day the Hindenburg Went Down," "Blobs, Spots, Specks, Smudges…," "Rejecting the Sargent-Welch Scientific Company's Measuring Kit in Mr. M.'s Physics Lab," and "Mr. M. and Mr. H. Talk over Lunch." The last two poems also appear in *2001: A Science Fiction Poetry Anthology,* ed. Keith Allen Daniels (Anamnesis Press, 2001).

"To Look at Any Thing" from *The Living God,* © 1961 by John Moffitt and renewed 1989 by Henry Moffitt, reprinted by permission of Harcourt Inc.

Though it is clear to me at the outset that I will fail to acknowledge all the books, conversations, photos, essays, articles, and broadcasts that have somehow made their way into these poems, I would like nevertheless to mention those to which I am most consciously indebted. These include Freeman Dyson's *Disturbing the Universe*, K.C. Cole's *Sympathetic Vibrations*, Wendell Berry's "Getting along with Nature" in *Home Economics*, John Burroughs's essay "Science and Literature," Jacob Bronowski's essays, the editors and authors of the Eyewitness Science Series, Lewis Wolpert's *The Unnatural Nature of Science*, Isaac Asimov's *Biographical Encyclopedia of Science and Technology*, Barbara Novak's *Nature and Culture: American Landscape Painting, 1825–1875*, D'Arcy Thompson's *On Growth and Form*, Dudley Young's *Origins of the Sacred: The Ecstasies of Love and War*, Roger S. Jones's *Physics as Metaphor* and *Physics for the Rest of Us*, William F. Lynch's *Christ and Apollo: The Dimensions of the Literary Imagination*, J. Robert Oppenheimer's lecture entitled "Physics in the Contemporary World," Robert Osserman's *Poetry of the Universe: A Mathematical Exploration of the Cosmos*, Wilczek and Devine's *Longing for the Harmonies*, John D. Barrow's *The Origin of the Universe*, the August 9, 1995 PBS broadcast entitled *The Day after Trinity*, James Gleick's *Chaos: Making a New Science*, Paul Johnson's *The Birth of the Modern*.

In addition, my thanks go to Joseph Enzweiler, poet and physics major, my friend and advisor in this project; to Chris Meyer, who introduced me to the physicist Dr. Sergey Grinshpun and his wife Dr. Vicky Appatova, who were the first informal audience for some of these poems; to David and Sally Stratman for their support and encouragement during the time these poems were taking shape, and over whose dinner table some of them were first voiced; to Janis Kennedy, my principal and reference at the time I applied for the Council for Basic Education grant; and to Terri Ford and Jim Palmerini, organizers of the poetry readings at the York Street International Cafe in Newport, Kentucky. In addition, I am grateful for the Poetry in the Park series in Columbus, Ohio; The Poetry Forum at Larry's in Columbus, Ohio; Joseph-Beth Booksellers in Cincinnati, Ohio; and for the Purcell Marian High School Open Mike Poetry Readings, where early versions of some of these poems were first read in public. I would also like to thank those advanced physics students in the class of 1995 at Purcell Marian in Cincinnati who so openly shared their frustrations and enthusiasms and their poems about physics with me during our time together. I likewise have gratitude for COSI, the Center of Science and Industry in Columbus, Ohio, where I first got hands-on experience with the harmonic cantilever. I give great thanks to Lucille Clifton, judge of the 1996 Pablo Neruda Prize in Poetry, in which a selection of these poems was named First Honorable Mention. The sequence entitled "Essay of the Body as Cloud Chamber" was a Finalist for the same prize in 1999. Lastly, and most especially, I thank the Council for Basic Education, which together with the NEA and the J. Paul Getty Center for Education in the Arts, granted me a 1995 Arts in Education Fellowship expressly for this project. It is because of their support that this book has come into being.

Contents

Preface & Apologia

The idea for a collection of poems about physics first struck me in October of 1994 as I was working with Creative Writing students at school. Many of the workshop participants were taking Advanced Placement physics and calculus, and they were struggling. Their physics teacher was not an answer-giver, but rather an encourager of thought and discovery. This was somewhat frustrating to the students, used to having control over subject matter, and accustomed to teachers who would answer all of their questions. As I listened to their talk about the course, I suggested they write poems about physics, about the teacher, and about their own frustrations. I pressed pretty hard, and a dozen or so poems came. To encourage them, I too wrote poems about physics, and about the teacher, with whom I had struck up a lunch-time relationship, and with whom I shared many of the writing students. He told me stories about what went on in class, and about his students' habits, and I began to write poems from a student's point of view, remembering my own physics class twenty-five years before, and imagining how—well, how dry physics could be when taught from a strictly classical, Newtonian point of view. Push-pull forces, acceleration, inertia, levers, winches, screws, and so on—how sometimes so boring (at least to the speaker of "Rejecting the Sargent-Welch Measuring Kit in Mr. M.'s Physics Lab"); how mechanical, lifeless, and humdrum. Thus in the writing I turned to the more exciting and more strange aspects of physics—and that led eventually to a significant cluster of poems which deal with the quantum realm, where the laws of classical physics are suspended or replaced by other laws which are so counter-intuitive as to appear nonsensical. Rich territory. That was where I spent most of my time my time reading and writing over the summer.

Though I could not resist starting my reading much earlier—my first notebook entry is dated April 19—I began my official five-week project on June 19 with Lewis Wolpert's *The Unnatural Nature of Science*. Wolpert is an apologist for the "privileged knowledge" of science—those most esoteric areas where science claims that only extremely sophisticated mathematics can come close to describing nature (and so implying that only those initiated into the knowledge of higher mathematics can speak the language of the world). Along the way, Wolpert attempts to dispose of the mythic imagination as a way of understanding nature:

> While myths do provide explanations to questions about "how and why," they are defective from at least two points of view: the problem being addressed may not be explicit, and the proposed solution may rest on arbitrary assumptions whose applicability is not specified.

I was later to find several equally reputable physicists who pointed out that the assumptions modern science are based on are often as "arbitrary" as those Wolpert dismisses (for example this, from *Physics for the Rest of Us*, by Roger Jones: "Quantum theory raises doubts about one of the most deeply held articles of scientific faith—the belief in an objective world that is independent of our observations.") Ah, an argument. As Sherlock Holmes was fond of saying, "The game was afoot."

So I studied quantum theory and modern cosmology and some strange nooks of mathematics (always from a layman's point of view; as one of the poems indicates, I have little math and no calculus), trying to feel my way into the world they described. Typically, I read hard for three hours in the morning, taking notes (over 100 pages by the end of the formal five week period), and then wrote for four hours in the afternoon. The writing period was a time of synthesis and re-reading over notes; frequently I would become frustrated with the physicists' claim that there was no clear verbal way to describe the world they saw, and I would try to do it for them. Or I would get so caught up in the reading and note-taking that I would neglect the afternoon's writing. So on June 23 I reminded myself in my notebook: "Poems first, physics second."

After a couple of weeks I saw that the poems I was writing were beginning to coalesce into two or three categories: poems from a young student's point of view, poems about discoveries leading to the atomic bomb, and poems about oddities and strangenesses at the edges of physics, mathematics, and the emerging study of Chaos Theory. I made a tentative plan for the book at that point: it would consist of three sections, and I began thinking of titles for each of them while searching out appropriate quotations from the literature to introduce the themes of each section to the reader.

And I kept writing and reading. A book I had salvaged from our school library's annual purging became critically useful to me: Isaac Asimov's *Biographical Encyclopedia of Science and Technology*. A number of serendipitous discoveries arose as a result of my having that book at hand, one of them crucial to finding the unifying motif for the bomb section, "Water Into Fire." It's a good story, characteristic of the delightful unexpectedness of the journey toward the book, and underscores, I think, the benefits of artists being willing to live with ambiguity and uncertainty—perhaps even courting it, for its surprises and revelations. Not having too detailed an agenda or plan when embarking on a project of discovery is a good thing, though only a few scientists might be willing to accept that: too messy, variables not taken into account, hard to quantify the results, etc. Still, here it is.

June 26:
Still trying to find a "beginning" poem—this morning the Whitmanesque poem, set after Whitman walks out of the lecture described in his poem "When I Heard the Learn'd Astronomer."

But then this serendip (or Jungian synchronicity):

Looking [in the aforementioned *Asimov's Biographical Encyclopedia*] for scientists alive at the same time as Whitman, I look first at Darwin. As I am reading the entry on him. I see this:

HMS Beagle was about to set out for a voyage of scientific exploration in

14

*1831 and Darwin was offered the post of ship's naturalist, after the fashion
of Brown a half century before and Banks a quarter century earlier still.*

Who's this Brown fellow? So I go to the entry on "Brown, Robert, Scottish
Botanist" and read this:

> *The second discovery had startling repercussions quite outside the field of the
> life sciences, a development that Brown himself could scarcely have foreseen. It
> resulted from his rather routine investigation of plant pollen.*
>
> *In 1827 as he was viewing a suspension of pollen in water under
> the microscope, he noted that the individual grains were moving about
> irregularly…*
>
> *This has since been called "Brownian motion" and Brown could merely
> report the observation. He had no explanation for it…*
>
> *…It was the first evidence for atomism that was an observation rather
> than a deduction.*

And so a poem playing around with Whitman and electricity and an idle
thought or hunch that something might come of it sends me to history of
science, and reveals a series of connections—Brownian motion—the water
vapor of Wilson's cloud chamber [run across at about this same time in
my reading]—the deuterium (heavy water) necessary to the Los Alamos
project. [And of course all this remembers the alchemist's ultimate goal of
transmuting elements—and it is here in my notes, for the first time, that I
have scribbled down as a possible section title "Water into Fire."]

And so it goes throughout the notebook—one thing unexpectedly
leading to another, connections occurring, writing arising out of them.
One other connection that could not have been predicted was the cloud
motif in "Water into Fire." Years ago, in another context, I read Barbara
Novak's wonderful book on nineteenth-century American painting,
Nature and Culture. As I was reading about Wilson's cloud chamber (the
first invention to allow the direct observation and study of subatomic
reactions), I remembered that the treatment of clouds and the sky was an

important issue among some nineteenth-century painters, both in America and in Europe. That led me to a footnote concerning the first scientific classifier of clouds, and that led to some connections between water, vapor, clouds, and the nuclear cloud. In a sense, the subject was waiting for me, because wherever I looked after that, I saw references to clouds among the physicists and chaos scientists; for example, Rabi's comments included in the epigraphs page of "Water into Fire," and the interesting background fact that Mitchell Feigenbaum, one of the fathers of Chaos Science, used up a great deal of one of his grants in paying for plane flights so that he could study the shapes and scales and edges of clouds.

In short, I saw again that what is true about any adventure—"expect the unexpected"—was again revealing itself. To paraphrase someone else, 'the subject was discovering itself to me.' There is hardly any higher intellectual or aesthetic pleasure than that.

It is just such excitement and joy that I try to let my students in on: besides reading a selection of the poems in physics class this year, I have shared my notebook with them, showing what a mess it looks like at first, but then how it begins to come together, and how one thing leads to another, even though there may be dead ends along the way. Keep on moving. Build it and they (sense and joy) will come.

On a more technical level, I found myself having to deal, in poems, with direct quotations from scientific and biographical materials. Could I incorporate such passages into the poems without breaking the voice the poems spoke in? An interesting problem; whether I've succeeded or not I'm not sure.

But overall, the pleasure and discovery of learning and writing in a subject matter dramatically different from the poems of place and natural detail typical of my work up until now was liberating. I found myself testing the theory of writing to learn and writing across the curriculum expressed in William Zinnser's *Writing to Learn*: that writing is a way of learning a subject, a way of making the subject your own, a way of moving forward into the unknown.

The limitations of the poems are very clear to me. I still do not speak

the language of mathematics; I still do not pretend to understand most of
the counter-intuitive "facts" of modern physics; I still may not have found a
language sufficient unto the subject. But perhaps I have reaffirmed a couple
of issues: that the pursuit of knowledge is indeed sometimes a Faustian
bargain ("Water into Fire"); that the "privileged" nature of scientific
knowledge needs to be looked at critically ("First Approach," "The Narrow
Gate"); that there is a terrible beauty in science, as in many other endeavors
of the mind and heart; that poetry and science share the habit of pressing
the edges of things (*At the Boundary*); that the richness of science may not be
entirely inaccessible to the artist, and that it may be a good idea for artists
to risk entering the precincts of science, even if they're found at last to be
fools. (A large possibility: even a renowned physicist, after presenting a
theory to Pauli, of The Pauli Exclusion Principle fame, said, "But surely,
Pauli, you don't think what I've said is completely wrong? To which Pauli
replied, "No, I think what you said is *not even wrong*.")

Nevertheless, one final medley from my notebook:

June 23
　　What is happening as I read and see once again how many
areas of study are inter-linked and interdependent is that there is
a whole "ecology" of knowledge—and as I see the impossibility
of "knowing it all," I have to resist the temptation to fall back
into my own little specialty, whatever that is—literature? poetry?
writing?—and (to use a metaphor that would have been nonsense
fifteen years ago, before the advent of the personal computer
and the software that drives it) keep many windows open, even
though the rage for connection and synthesis might never be
satisfied. Perhaps one difference between the artist and the
scientist—at least when they are most intensely in their "official
capacities"—is that the artist deliberately courts ambiguity and
uncertainty; he or she has a willingness, if not an outright need,
to dwell in Negative Capability, and to trust that "something will

happen."

Glancing up as I was a while ago admiring D'Arcy
Thompson's prose, especially his description of an amoeba, I
saw on the bookshelf Dudley Young's *Origins of the Sacred*, and it
came powerfully to me that I might need to balance the heavy
particularity and "factness" of all I am reading with something
more mythic, even mystical like *Origins*. I'm strongly tempted to
do just that—to read it as an anodyne against too much of what
Thoreau called "mere fact."

July 10
[from *Origins of the Sacred*]: A scientific 'fact' might be called a tale
without a teller. We believe Einstein's stories not because he tells
them while dressed in a purple robe, but because $E=mc^2$ looks
good on everybody's slide rule. This 'democratic' simplicity,
objectivity, and universality are science's great strengths, but
also its great weakness. A tale without a teller has no author, is
not authorized, lacks authority; like a foundling in our midst it
stands unconnected to us, without relation, unpredictable. Not
named within the circle of our human bonds, this foundling
may be monstrous. Who was to say $E=mc^2$ would turn into an
atomic bomb? Certainly not Einstein, the unfathering father, full
of remorse. What makes this story monstrous is that it tells us
where to find power, but is silent about when and where to use
it. This silence, which claims to be high-minded, in fact allows
unspeakable desires to slip from the shadows. Like a violent,
psychotic child, this equation carries power without either self-
control or the restraining hand of its father's law. Such power is
intrinsically chaotic.

Working that summer on these poems, wrestling with issues of
knowledge and power, facing technical challenges in the poems themselves,
pushing forward into more and more unfamiliar territory, I was constantly

brought face to face with limitation: the limits of language, the limits of imagination, the limits of sympathy and identification. At the same time, though, I felt confirmed in my feeling that the artist, when his or her inclinations so lead, ought to participate along with the scientist in the unfolding quest. Dialogue between the arts and the sciences is a way in which the truth of nature can be approached, however strange, beautiful, dangerous, contradictory, and ultimately mysterious truth—and nature—may be.

Prologue

The chief interest of mankind in nature or in the universe can never be for any length of time a merely scientific interest.

—John Burroughs, "Science and Literature"

Worldword

Beginning at the quasar-riddled world's edge,
twelve billion light-years in the distance,
(that is, twelve billion light-years in the past)
far beyond what Homer could have dreamed back to,
far beyond the world-edge outcast Cain or Grendel roamed,
stranger than the door somewhere in ancient Ur
where Gilgamesh slips through to underworld—
though *edge*, or *end* or *under* are not the words
to name it, for it is edgeless, unending, and
neither under or over but
curved there and herethere and therehere—

But at the edge of what we see,
at the edge of what we say and cannot say,
dance or cannot dance,
sing or cannot sing,
begins and ends a story
that both re-tells and invents itself.

To begin, the story needs time,
and so invents it,
then remembers to start itself.

It needs language, nomination and annunciation,
and so invents them,
to name and call and know itself.

It needs space to grow in,
and so invents it,
inflating in the very time it has made and is made of,

muttering in every burst and curl and twist
of energy and time its name,
blooming brightly, darkly,
grainily, smoothly, ever enfolding,
ever unreeling.

It needs a receiver of the same shape
as its meaning and its name,
a receiver infinite and finite,
small and large,
both matter and spirit,
many and one,
locus of the quantum and classical,
and so invents it,
(it is what invents this poem)
—the invention
inventing itself—
all out of nothing—
all out of the nothing, itself—

itself nothing
but named, by itself,
into something.

Something spoken: named: announced:
something invented, something springing
out of itself that was nothing.

Gravity, strong and weak forces;
matter, fusion,
harmony and dissonance, destruction and birth,
hadrons, hummingbirds, hostas:
darkness and light:

darkness toothed and winged like a dragon,
light pierced and crucified,
piercing and crucifying like God:
complexity unfolding and unlooping
then curving back in on itself,
spiral of the ammonite, Fibonnaci's Sequence
informing its curving and growth,
Henle's Loops,
alveoli, the haunting paisleys of chaos,
space motherly and strange,
bringing forth the alien and familiar home of all.

And so forming, growing, changing,
it needs tension, push-pull, suspense,
forces all, and invents them,
and at the same time mystery,
the greatest force of all,
calling all to it as
nectar the bee, light the gyring moth,
sex the procreant cell.

It needs loveliness and form,
connectedness, grace, unity,
flow and dance,
and so invents them.

In the beginning it is the word
and the world
all word forms and then inhabits:

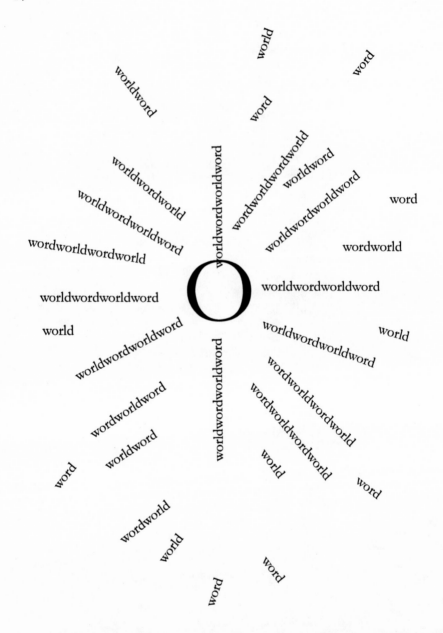

The Self Electric, Whitmanesque, Shapes up along Lines of Force

"Electricity is not a thing, like St. Paul's Cathedral; it is a way in which
things behave."
—Bertrand Russell

Having just stepped out
"to look up in perfect silence at the stars,"
having just remembered that in any beginning
"is the Word,"
having listened to Ginsberg's "Sunflower Sutra"
with its blossom and locomotive,
its marriages of soul and machine,
power and spirit,
here and now and there and forever,
having labored amid vocabularies vast
as any body, and as beautiful,
I step out, reader, hoping you will step
out with me, seekingly with me:

Field, influence, harmonic venturing:
I find I spread myself wider and higher,
find that I am pulling myself into existence
"by my own bootstraps,"
the gravity of my curiosity bending spacetime
towards me, capturing all, eating it as if prey

in delight's digestion and transformations,

And so I grow out toward edges, shores, clearings,
eddies aside from the current but
still remembering and driven by its flow,
transition zones,
frontiers, borders,
places where form and phase
begin to transform:
I seek out the dance of All,
seek out whirl and spin and
that old god Proteus,
father of bold Kinesis,
father of that beauty Turbulence.

I want to dance the tarantella
with his daughters,
(they are my daughters, too,
beautiful thoughts and hunches),
play the chord for hydrogen,
sing the spectrum of neon,
occupy the cloudy realm of electrons,
hover and swoop and
blink like neutrino in and out,
on and off, being and not-being,
explore the worm-holed grainy basement
of things, crunch the time-stuff underfoot
like the gravel from matter's flood,
look out over it all smiling and
cry, "We're home."

I want to hug unto myself
all children, dreams, poems, curses,
and smile, enlarge, dilate, discourse and deliver,

and then puff them all toward heaven
like the nimbus of dandelion.

Student jocular, intuitive, irregular,
scholar-father wild and impertinent,
mother-physicist of the improbable and invisible unfinished,
cousin mechanical of the line and syllogism and seed,

I follow along,
seeking my work through the dust ahead,
(O what great destruction, there,
what dark stories, what explosions?)
seeking physics through the growth and scrub of time,
hearing always its music
like singing far down in the woods,
that trough of moist darkness and hours,
hearing always its music high up on the ridge,
that crest in the slow wave of land,
hearing it even now
in the astronomer's charts and numbers,
in her tallys of force and speed,
and in harvest's first shoots and leaves:

I see now
I have been fitted to this energy and flow,
its case and premises my flesh,
its terminals and summations
my eyes and ears and fingers.

I am potent, ready.
I am its battery and array,
its brief and argument,

its load and spark and signal:

I await your telling discharge of me, cosmos,
physics,
O my soul.

The more I examine the universe and study the details of its architecture,
the more evidence I find that the universe in some sense must have known
that we were coming.

—Freeman Dyson, *Disturbing the Universe*

First Approach

Poetry is at once the center and circumference of knowledge; it is that which comprehends all science, and that to which all science must be referred.

—Shelley, "A Defense of Poetry"

Some truth meets the eye. Some does not. We are up against a mystery.

—Wendell Berry, "Letter to Wes Jackson"

All science is the search for unity in hidden likenesses, and the starting point is an image, because then the image is before the mind's eye.

—Jacob Bronowski, "The Reach of the Imagination"

O nature, and O soul of man! how far beyond all utterance are your linked analogies.

—*Moby Dick*

Be humble for you are made of dung. Be noble for you are made of stars.

—Old Serbian proverb

Non coerci maximo, contineri tamen a minimo. [Not to be hemmed in by the largest and yet to be contained in the smallest].

—St. Ignatius Loyola

Beginning Physics with Mr. M.

Craziness
on Monday,
in the buzzing lab,
fish, birds, rodents—
as if biology were physics
("It is, of course," says Mr. M.),
—he hands each of us an owl-pellet,
then a pan and needle.
After he explains,
much sniffing,
scowls, denial.
"Out of control!"
"Get real!"
"I won't take this crap!"

"Look.
Dissect.
Note and mark.
Imagine.
Record and reconstruct."
—All Mr. M. will say.

On Tuesday,
I think of the dusty histories
of shrews and mice,
sudden swirls of wind
on an edged and tricky night
above the meadow,
the warmth of blood
trickling from a mouth.

On Wednesday,
I breathe in dust
blown up from my pan
and pellet.
I taste urine, decay,
burnt hair.

On Thursday,
I feel my shoulders broaden,
my face collapse,
grown narrower and beaked.
I see minutely
far across the room.

Then Mr. M is here, transformed,
keen-eyed, calm and constant as
all the principles of algebra,
compact and terse as Newton,

and reads John Moffit's poem
"To Look At Any Thing":

To look at any thing,
If you would know that thing,
You must look at it long:
To look at this green and say
'I have seen spring in these
Woods' will not do—you must
Be the thing you see:
You must be the dark snakes of
Stems and ferny plumes of leaves,
You must enter in

To the small silences between
The leaves,
You must take your time
And touch the very peace
They issue from.

Friday,
I hardly know myself.
Trees miles away
come suddenly to mind.
My head swivels smoothly
from side to side.

Across the room
a lab rat stares at me
and crouches,
nervous in its cage.

What we call an isolated particle is in reality the product of its interaction with its surroundings. It is therefore impossible to separate any part of the universe from the rest.

—Fritjof Kapra

In a Collective Nightmare, Mr. M. Instructs The Whole Class: "Just Smile and Nod"

If I tell you that physics is poetry,
just smile and nod.

If I tell you it is only in physics
that we can begin to understand
the shape of God, the heft of her form,
the subtlety of her body,
just smile and nod.

If I tell you that there is nothing more
beautiful than physics,
and that suffering is beauty,
just smile and nod.

If I tell you in the first photograph
of an atomic bomb, a split-second
into its explosion, God's face appeared,
appalled, in the fireball,
just smile and nod.
Like you,
I did not believe these things at first.

Mr. M. Accelerates

Mr. M. stands at the board,
a diagram of the universe
behind him. "Do not think
it is contained," he warns,
pointing at the border
of the slate. "Indeed, it goes on,
continuing to accelerate
from its center,
which, like Nicholas of Cusa's God,
is everywhere
and nowhere."

I grip my desktop,
suddenly furious with stillness.
I want to catch up,
accelerate past the
Big Bang, get out
in front of its expansion
and ride like a surfer
the very break and plunge
of energy into matter,

hang ten into infinity,
catch up with Mr. M.,
who seems to stand still
before us in class, twirling his chalk,
but who secretly hotdogs it
high on the curl of All,
then laughs in the roar
of the Nothing or Everything

he pipelines,
out there way beyond us.

...Is not liberty, much more than the intelligence, the faculty of the
possible, a "movement that goes beyond" and a negation of limitations?
Non coerci maximo. On the other hand, the more distant and extraordinary is
its goal the more it must locate itself in the most immediate and the most
proximate if it is to reach or move toward this goal. *Contineri a minimo.*

—William F. Lynch, *Christ and Apollo: The Dimensions of the Literary Imagination*

Mr. M. and Mr. H. Talk over Lunch

Mr. M. allows as how
the other night
he required
his AP physics students to
take their books
to the poetry reading
at Kaldi's Coffeehouse.

Mr. H. says he thought he'd
felt something strange there;
he'd hypothesized at the time
low barometric pressure
and high humidity. "Now I see
it was a kind of friction," he says,
"set up between the laws of physics
and the freedom of poetry."

"No problem there," Mr. M. says.
"As you well know yourself,
the laws of physics may be suspended
in the vicinity of the poem."

"True enough," Mr. H. says.
"But there is always residual noise
caused by the presence of physics,
which mutters constants to itself,
even on the cosmic scale.
It is over this
background noise
that poetry has to raise its voice."

H. and M. fall silent,
mulling the poetry of the very moment,
its obedience to the laws that predict
that something, given time, will happen
—and it does:

Outside, over the DeSales Lane sidewalk,
a squirrel ungrounded, as if leaping across the sky,
travels surely and unharmed
along the rainslicked vector of a power line—

An event, they agree,
very like a poem.

BriefLecture on the Oscillating Universe

"Let me put it this way,"
Mr. M. says. "Out is in."

Rejecting The Sargent-Welch Scientific Company's Measuring Kit in Mr. M.'s Physics Lab

I do not even open it,
Pandora's Box of fixity and stillness:
number shackles, bondages of relation,
skewed angles of repose.
Instead, I measure the length of class
by how many shapes the clouds
assume over the cityscape outside:
weasel, camel, humpback whale.
I measure the angle of the azimuth
by the syllables of memory and body:
something is one Susan high,
something else my Desolina low,
a third exactly as long as the silent fall
of Cindy's silken panties.

—O so quickly and privately gone
from lecture and equation,
shot at imagination's hot velocities,
flesh-changer, time-bender,
space-warper through daydream's slick wormholes,

I meet myself at the horizon of heaven,
where simmer Nature's molten landscapes,
rises, slopes, secret rills
of the honeyed sweat
down the Venus of her presence,

But then just as quickly
am ripped back, the smell of blistered paint
scorching on the radiator,
some nerd across the lab
coughing, asthmatic, tubercular,
ratcheting sputum into a filthy tissue—
all the besmeared, jaundiced, pimpled,
knock-kneed, bad-breathed
here:

And so I remember the flagellate I once saw
aswirl in a spot of pond on a slide:
all the filamentous oars of that diamond
boat its body,
excited and alive in its
halo of motion and uncertainty—
Ernst Abbe's "disc of light"—

Its glassy self
encrystalled like a geode,
evanescing at its edges into space,
spinning marvelous in an ether
unmeasurable
save in degrees of absolute
beauty.

BriefDis ofPhysics

Frankly, I don't give a fig, Newton.

The Narrow Gate

Most of us are in daily contact with at least as much that we do not understand as were the Greeks or early Babylonians.

—Frank Oppenheimer

In fact, everything we know is only some kind of approximation, because we know that we do not know all the laws yet. Therefore, things must be learned only to be unlearned again, or, more likely, corrected.

—Richard Feynman

There is an external world separable from our perception.
The world is rational: 'A' is not equal to 'not A.'
The world can be analysed locally—that is, one can examine a process without having to take into account all the events occurring elsewhere.
There are regularities in nature.
The world can be described by mathematics.
These presuppositions are universal.

—Physicist John Barrow on the assumptions of modern science; quoted in
The Unnatural Nature of Science by Lewis Wolpert

Quantum theory raises doubts about one of the most deeply held articles of scientific faith—the belief in an objective world that is independent of our observations.

—Roger Jones, *Physics for the Rest of Us*

Mild cosmic paranoia seems to be a fruitful attitude.

—Wilczek and Devine, *Longing for the Harmonies*

The Narrow Gate

He approaches,
principles and laws in his pocket like folded maps,
a basic vocabulary ticking in his head
like a small, watch-like black box
telling time and space.

And no other way into this world
but through this humming arbor, garlanded
with bunched roses of velocity, canes
of vector and momentum,
pinpoint thorns of the Planck Time.

—As forbidden to him
as the center of Eden.
Still, he wants to see what's up,
(and has no notion that "up"
and "down" and "east" and "west"
are, hereafter, meaningless.)
Only numbers, he has been told,
can give directions here.

But to him, all he approaches
is mute, and beyond it, the spacetime enclosed
within the "walls" the gate passes through,
murmur vast integers and fractions,
all properties of matter,
all rules and laws of physics:
the Pauli Exclusion Principle,
Quantum Mechanics,

the Special and General Theories
of Relativity.

Other problems as well:
constants, for example;
the endurance of pi,
the virginal constancy
of c, the famous speed of light,
the minuscule but powerful and absolutely
inflexible value of the Planck Length
and the barely-possible trickery
of the Planck Time.

And even more:
the problem of "length" or
"position" or "velocity"—
the conundrums at the base
of the measurement of anything—
here are all contained and revealed,

and here he will struggle,
as if attempting to build a pyramid
with no way to make a corner square—
with no way even to
know the notion "corner."

And more awaits within: the lives of physicists,
thousands of them, their eyes
exhibiting all the colors of the spectrum,
their hands outlined with blue sparks,
their hair standing wildly upright
as if they lean on Van deGraf generators,
their words intense and charged as

the climbing arcs of Jacob's Ladders—
and too their dreams, the states of their digestions
and knees and lungs,
and too, clinging to them
like confetti to staticky trousers,
chance, ignorance,
forces, powers, appointments and demotions,
and along with them
brilliance and stupidity,
apocalyptic angels riding the same dark horse,
and too their multiple marriages of the visible and invisible,
the soap operas and tragedies of their laboratory affairs,
and too rage and envy and murder and awful glory.

All this hubbub our pilgrim approaches,
blind, unequipped,
speaking in only grunts and squeals
while approaching the Empire of Mathematics.

No calculus.
Little algebra.
Even as he comes nearer,
the gate grows narrower and narrower.
So he decreases, too,
ashamed at his own arrogance,
realizing his silly self-assumptions,
but shrugs, grins like the Cheshire Cat,
becomes almost a point,
and passes through
into what at first
he cannot see or say.

Maybe he's in heaven:
but even money says,
for him,
all hell is breaking loose.

The Place Where There Is No Between

I can only say, there we have been: but I cannot say where.
And I cannot say, how long, for that is to place it in time.

—T.S. Eliot, *Four Quartets*

Trying to get his bearings
in this suddenly stranger world,
with its up and down, its spin and charm,
directions, possibilities of being
never known to him before,
he sees that all is moving,
humming, vibrating,
that the whole universe is
a kind of resonance and harmony,
though exactly *what* kind of harmony,
nor of what that harmony is made,
he cannot say.

Even language folds into itself
in odd places, revealing a kind of rhyme:
he learns that arithmetic
(—*a one and a two and a three...*)
and rhythm
(*doo-wop-she-bop*)
come from the same Greek root,
the word "to flow."
Numbers flow,
music flows,
meter flows,
the lines of his former homeplace flowed.

And he thinks it's beginning
to make sense:
flow is how the poem happens,
the image coalescing gradually,
the words shaping themselves out of
sight and sound
into sight and sound,
the event unfolding and exposing itself
until it becomes clear to itself and to him.
Flow is the line emerging from silence
into meaning and song,
flow the painter's line looping into form
and color incarnating into shape—
flow, he sees, is how all happens,
how all accomplishes, fulfills.
Flow is how the calculus proceeds,
flow the times table,
flow all real numbers,
flow how time and space are—
flow is harmony, flow the sine wave,
flow all that is graceful and dance-like in creation.

No.

All: chocolate, whiskey,
watch oil, fog: all
in this new place is not smooth,
not pudding or molasses:
all is grainy, interrupted:
there is, at the most fundamental level,
an indivisibility to things,
(even, perhaps, to time):

grittiness, not elasticity,
gravelly discreteness, not honeyed fluidity:
not silk, but ratchets,
not wheels, but toothed gears,
not clarinet smears, but only sharp single notes—
not flow but leappauseleap:
the dancer is not gliding here then
pirouetting slowly there—
she is here, or there:
there is no in between.

Immediately, he perceives with dread
his real position:
in this new place,
he will stay forever behind
the fact, forever stranger to what is true
until (and if) he has learned enough,
accumulated enough energy,
electron-like,
to leap to the new understanding.

No.

Only on the tiniest levels of things and events
is there no between.
In most worlds of the size he is fitted to,
there can be gradual progress, smooth,
though peaked and valleyed,
though halting and irregular:
moments of speed and moments of motionlessness,
moments of dance, and moments of rest.

And out of them, the poem occurs,

humming node fed by everything around it:
moments, instants, not-times, time-knots,
matters of fact and matters of fiction,
factions, fractions and fissions,

expansions and dilations,
wild escapes, intimate rubbings-up-against,

ins and outs,
ups and downs,
not-down un-ups,
even making place somehow for in between.

From the swings of pendulums,
flooding and ebbing tides, orbits,
heartbeats, seasons,
beautiful backs-and-forths,

the poem forms
what worldword says:

*Do wop she bop
and a one and a two and a three*

Where Algebra Is No Help

Veiled, wimpled, smelling of talcum
and a bitter, lemony grace,
black rosary beads clacking at her sides,
Sr. Eileen in high school algebra class,
after the *Our Father, who art in heaven,*
anchoring us
solidly in time and place
and reminding us of our dull, sublunary status,
first showed him the Commutative Principle,

$$A \times B = B \times A$$

The month of his birth, 8,
times the day of his birth, 7
equals 56, and so, too, vice versa,
every time: one of the eternal rules
of how numbers work.

But here where there is
no between,
common numbers are amiss.
He learns about quaternions,
studied by William Rowan Hamilton,
friend of Coleridge and Wordsworth.
Hamilton builds an algebra
logical only when

$$B \times A = -A \times B.$$

What application of this madness
in the world? None, it seems,
for three-quarters of a century.
Then, "a noncommutative algebra
was to form the basis
for quantum mechanics...
for the proper understanding
of the internal structure
of the atom."

Strangeness, nonsense.
At night in his new world
he wakes sweating and afraid,
ridden with fever-visions:
clouds and fire.
He studies the body of panic,
wild in the bed beside him.

And all in this place
is aswirl and ashimmer,
his room no longer square,
but evolving into some new shape
in new dimensions,

his body folded and collapsed
within it, all incurve, swoop, contortion,
rubbery orphan of iron-handed topology,

and nowhere is there a there
that, once leaving (if he could),
he can find his way back to.

Up By Its Bootstraps, or Tongue of Chameleon
As a Slice of Field

In cartoons, where the laws of physics
are regularly suspended,
craziness happens: Coyote flies out over the chasm,
stops dismayed, mugs forlornly a few seconds in mid-air,
then falls with a declining whine,
(the Doppler Effect still a great gag to all of us)
and hits bottom in a small explosion
only later followed by the puff of smoke:
sound traveling faster than light.
Then, a moment later,
Coyote does it all again:
resurrection of the trickster,
divine anarchic stupidity
outlasting entropy and wreckage—
energy and matter constantly recreated.

Or inertia is denied: the Roadrunner
doing eighty down the desert highway
beep beeps and stops, literally,
on a dime, and survives unharmed,
brain not smashed flat inside its skull,
internal organs still all
in their places
though instantly decelerated:
in the real world, we're talking
spleen and liver mashed against the ribs
like tomato paste,
brains like a plate full of hummus

tossed against the front wall of the skull.
But in cartoons, anything is possible:
it's why we laugh. Something
there is that doesn't love a law,
that says, "I can hit that wall and live."

But reality, we know,
is dense, unforgiving, recalcitrant:
algebra's solutions,
chemistry's immutable formulae,
concussion's insensate face
when we hit the pole.
Things happen; causes and effects (and semicolons)
exist; we live to state, relate and prove.

Like the "Bootstraps Theory," for example.
As in "pulling yourself up by the bootstraps."
Picture that, literally, for a moment;
draw it, if you can,
in this space:

—A cartoon notion, if there ever was one.
But for some physicists, as reasonable as any.

They say, for example, that light propagates through space
something like the weird unfolding tongue
of the chameleon stretching into air.
Chameleon sees prey, grows excited, launches forth—
its weird mouth flapping open,
loosing a kind of slobbery awning
that unfolds to nab some fly and wetly wrap around it.

Now, subtract the chameleon:
leave only the tongue,
unfolding out of itself
endlessly in mid-air,
and this not only in one direction,
but according to probability, in any
direction at once:
some sort of joke.

But in the subatomic world,
says physics,
it just goes on and on,
pulling itself into existence
"by its own bootstraps,"
unfolding out of the field
it propagates of itself,
as if feet create with their every step
the very world they tread on.

And sober and in all seriousness,
physics claims,
offering as proof
its laws and numbers and QEDs,
that there's no Coyote here.

What we have said for photons goes for electrons, or other 'particles,' too.
Each is described by its own field, a medium filling all space that, when
excited, gives birth to the particle.

—Wilczek and Devine, *Longing for the Harmonies*

Elementary, My Dear Watson

1
Maybe once, sometime,
when human beings still hunted mammoths,
crushing them in pits with
boulders flung
in the birth of ballistics,

maybe then, when the groan of ice receding
toward the North accompanied the first poems,
chants of deliverance
from cold and darkness,
set to pulse's and breathing's rhythms,

maybe then a rock was a rock—
all there, substance complete,
kickable without philosophizing,
an event immediate and simple,
pain spoken plainly from foot to brain,
as if all were one: rock, foot, pain,
and all as animate and god-filled as every other,
packed with meaning and immanence,
radiant with common song and ground.

But then the world,
pried by icy mind,
split, fractured,
fell apart.

Democritus:
"All is made of indivisibles,
nothing is smaller than them,
they are All, live forever,
cannot be lost or destroyed."

"Void is that
which is not these indivisibles."

Then Thales of Miletus:
"The world is made of water:
there are no divinities, no satyrs,
no guardian gods of the boundaries."
Man and nature and the divine
no longer whole:

swan and woman, thunder and man:

Apart: strangers for the first time.

2
Newton in the garden at Cambridge:
an apple falls (apple? the same one
as in the First Garden,
the same one we could not resist,
fruit of Knowledge, Power,
Godliness, Control:
the selfsame apple?)

And classical physics comes clear,
and all notions of movement,
and all reasons (it seems)

for how the universe works.
A great clockworks,
God the watchmaker,
nature the stuff
of the machine.

3
Thus the diminishment of mystery
and ascent of science
arrive with the mystery story
and decline then death of God:

Poe, attending feverishly and willy-nilly
the birth of the modern,
creates the first detective,
whose tools and cutting skills
sharpen and culminate in Holmes,
"priest of the invisible,"
chemist, observer, deducer,
explicator of nature's warps and vices,
bachelor Victorian detective,
egotistic tangle of Freudian knots
who armed with sense and mind and logic,
arrests the chaotic,
disciplines the clever malfeasant,
spanks mind and motive into shape,
a maniac of hypothesis,
dominating and controlling,
and so,
(at least until Szilard takes a walk in London
and imagines nuclear fission,
until Heisenberg tests his hunches,
until Einstein wakes all sleepers in a few small papers)

seems to solve, for all us foolish Watsons,
simply everything.

4

But now, a mess:

pions, muons, strange and up, charm and down,
spin, string theory, a hundred
particles more "elementary"
than the atom: and physics in a tizzy,
scrambling for names, surrounded
in a hum of wavicles and virtual particles
and buzzing frenzy
like men attacked by bees:

as if Moriarty, that old villain,
loosing a wild confusion
on a world of ordinary laws,
plunged over the Reichenbach Falls
and transformed before he struck the rocks,
returning wickedly as x-rays,
lightning bolts, deuterium;
as if every cow
in the Wessex pastures back home
were just a version, now,
of the orginal cosmic burn:
a kind of hoofed fuel,
a kind of chemical repetition,
a kind of ruminant, slow explosion.

Holmes: put that in your pipe
and smoke it.

At the Boundary

Many famous scientists have given advice: try many things; do what makes your heart leap; think big; dare to explore where there is no light; challenge expectation; *cherchez le paradox*; be sloppy so that something unexpected happens, but not so sloppy that you can't tell what happened; turn it on its head; never try to solve a problem until you can guess the answer; precision encourages the imagination; seek simplicity; seek beauty."

—Lewis Wolpert, *The Unnatural Nature of Science*

The rolling of eddies, the unfurling of ferns, the creasing of mountain ranges, the hollowing of animal organs all followed one path, as [Theodor Schwenk] saw it. It had nothing to do with any particular medium, or any particular kind of difference. The inequalities could be slow and fast, warm and cold, dense and tenuous, salt and fresh, viscous and fluid, acid and alkaline. At the boundary, life blossoms.

—James Gleick, *Chaos: Making a New Science*

Einstein knew that going to extremes of size or speed could lead to qualitatively surprising results. Throughout the history of science, the most fruitful areas for exploration have hovered at the extremes and fringes—the outer limits of hot and cold, fast and slow, big and small, few and many.

—K.C. Cole, *Sympathetic Vibrations*

Nothing interests us which is stark or bounded, but only what streams with life, what is an act or endeavor to reach somewhat beyond.

—Ralph Waldo Emerson

Energy Drains from the Poem

I work to square the line,
pack the right blackpowder verb
into meaning's ammunition, then fine-
tune the sights, and swerve-

less, steady as stone, drill the temple
of the giant Nonsense, kill Confusion,
bring to its knees with vorpal
word and snicker-snack of intention

all Unclarity. Win. Overcome.
With mass and speed and skill
whip the butts of
these bullies

doggone fellows with their
eyes
off-center,

cyclops

or titans
vam

pires!

sucking
away all

sense

and order

till before
I
know
it's

all   god   help

u   s g
on

e

Light

Tis here!
Tis here!
Tis gone!

—*Hamlet*, Act I, Scene 1

It moves in packets, discrete,
and is wrapped in the same stuff, after all,
that thought is wrapped in,
and that shrews are wrapped in, too,
in their heat and speed,
and is the latticed excitement
that strikes the wings of damselflies
over the pond at noon, motes
that catch and hold;
green bright eye of pasture.

It is wrapped tight,
neat fury minuscule
as love's first thrill
and tickle:

tender static
in the nerves of lips
approaching, in the stroked hair
brilliant, in the fingertip that sparks
along the soft way of the throat
or breast to home.

No. It is the sea,
dancing, wind mixing always,
rising and descending always,
crested and troughed,
packed, like thought,
with schools and shoals
of sense:
darters, gliders, dazzlers,
nudgers, strikers:
pearls and corals,
silts and ooze's
exhalations
rising.

Or both at once,
wave and particle,
dancing over everything we see,
streaming like an avalanche of wind,
or dust storm, mote-rain,
or turbulence smooth as swirled silk,

at once both whole and part,
visible and invisible,
everywhere and nowhere,
lingering as dusk does in the North,
yet abrupt as nightfall in the tropics:

even in our bedrooms,
it comes and goes,
guttering like a candle on the mantel.
As we kiss and sigh, we glance its way:

Now you see it,

now you

Extreme Sensitivity to Initial Conditions

You already know the story:
a small moth flaps its wings in Peking on Tuesday
and so on Friday there's a hurricane
in Miami. "The Butterfly Effect," it's called.
The little wind of the wings adds up,
sets off a series of "causally related"
reactions that, because of amplification effects
and the nature of chaos
result in huge consequences: as if to kiss a girl
were at once to beget a brigade.

Hell of a way to run a railroad.
Say I'm hit by a car right after I leave here
this evening. Anything I do right now
can't affect it; if I were
to change even one tiny thing—
go to the john right in the middle

of this poem, for example,
it wouldn't matter, because
it would have already been "built into"
the evening.
I can't surprise the future,
even if I can surprise myself.

Dropping the cereal box this morning
leads directly to my being hit later tonight.
Pausing to watch the beetle in the garden this morning:
just enough to bring me and the car together.

Drive a person crazy,
consciousness of all these little moments, causes,
and all their possible effects.

Close your eyes,
world seems to say.
All is Sarajevo,
under siege:

Run like hell—or stop.
Maybe you'll get there.
Maybe you won't.

The Day the Hindenburg Went Down

In many ways, the cause *is* that complex of circumstances—and it may
include everything from the day's weather to the full weight of history.

—K.C. Cole, *Sympathetic Vibrations*

The day before the Hindenburg went down
my grandfather was fleeing Germany.
It was cold, late spring,
sometimes snowing—
still, as he crossed
the river in the town of Koblenz,
the river that flowed on both sides
of a yellow house on an island,
he paused to watch the carp
near shore
nudge and suck the bottom.

Later that day,
high in the Bavarian mountains,
he hurried past a woman
in fox and sable, her hands
warm in a fur muff.
She was beautiful,
her chill, high cheekbones,
her vivid lips.
Her eye caught his; for a moment
the future of the whole world
tottered.

But—
Hitler loosed in his glancing away,
Nuremburg commenced, the ash of Hiroshima lit—
my grandfather hustled by, determined
in some universal hurry,
past the Roman ruins of Trier,
through the narrow gates of Rothenburg,
up the hills of Heidelburg,

Until at last, in late evening,
he boarded a great dirigible,
dim, huge, floating
like a cathedral moored to a sapling,
and fell, as if his work were over,
immediately to sleep.
In the hum of the tiny engine,
faint as a bee in a dream,
he was carried like a seed
over half of Europe in the night,
escaping, unharmed and smiling,
toward uncountable futures
the day the Hindenburg went down.

Peculiar Is as Peculiar Does

Something as peculiar as we find light to be can interact consistently only
with equally peculiar stuff.

—Frank Wilczek and Betsy Devine, *Longing for the Harmonies*

Stuff like the net inside my eye,
connected to strange gangly spiders
that eat the photons
captured in its red webbing
then transmit them to the brain
where, elegant and sharp,
they unfold somehow into meaning:
Oh, I see.

The German biologist Franz Boll
just happened to have in his cupboard
one afternoon
a fresh frog's eye.
Bringing it into the light to study,
he noticed that the redness
at its back quickly faded.
He returned it to the dark:
red again.
Oh, I see, Boll said.

Parable:
A man comes down the road
carrying a photon,
a kind of particle bomb.
It is wrapped loosely

in Uncertainty: no one knows
exactly what it is,
or exactly where it is at the same time:
it's in the package, somewhere,
probably—
don't look,
or it will be gone.
The man hands it to the great red spider
of the eyeway,
who eats it—
the little photon bomb explodes.
Naturally,
this makes the spider jump and dance,
kick little rods
filled with what
Boll saw: "visual scarlet."

This red stuff contains
a complex molecule called retinene,
shaped something like a bridge—
if one end of the bridge
has collapsed.

The proton blowing through
straightens the bridge out,
excites the visual scarlet
that brightens in the light.
(If too excited, though,
or for too long, it fades,
needs "resting" in the dark:
hence Boll's observation.)
Then, "By some means not understood"
this straightening out

in turn excites the nerve cells, which
send signals, via the optic nerves
and through the crossover
called the chiasma
into both sides of the brain.

There, "memory cells"—
one recognizing grandma,
another Uncle Albert,
another a rectangle moving horizontally
(but, strangely, not the same one moving vertically)
—fire
"in a manner yet to be discovered,"
—talk to one another
"in a manner yet to be discovered,"
—exchange information
"in a manner yet to be discovered,"
—and thereby "create perception,"
which is to say,
all the physicist perceives.
At the end of his lecture on quantum dynamics,
(nothing about sight or thought or perception),
the physicist turns away from the board
and smiles.
"See?" he asks, watching his students nod.

Oh, yes.
Right. Whatever.

Horatio: O but this is wondrous strange.
Hamlet: And therefore as a stranger give it welcome.
—*Hamlet*, act 1

Harmonic Cantilever: A Poetry Lesson

Poetry requires a certain fine balancing
  of not only sense and sound but of the stuff that is
    the world, stacked in lines so perfectly, so justly arranged
      as to hold themselves gracefully up with themselves and at
        the same time dance, even almost overdo it, but never fall.

Picasso Writes to Niels Bohr at Los Alamos

Thus the Cubist painting contains all the angles, all the impressions, all the possible views of a violin, brought to life at a single instant on the canvas.
—William F. Lynch, *Christ and Apollo: The Dimensions of the Literary Imagination*

My Dear Professor Bohr:

You say you see in my *Guernica*
the physics of horror,
dismemberment velocities,
vectors of violation.

You see real people, Professor,
minimized to accelerating blobs of tissue,
brain-smash, eye-burst, breast-explode.

You see how my painting
must accomplish all aspects and directions
at once, must be omnipresent like God
to trumpet its judgment and lamentation.

One cannot consider such horror
from the single vantage point only:
from all sides the event
cries out to be imagined, witnessed,
and remembered.

I have heard there may be other
such things going on:

Germany, Poland, Hungary—
I am sure you know what I mean.

And as above us in the sky clouds form,
condense, and dissipate, revealing
suns's flash and shape, dear Professor,
that which is unseen will be seen.

Box Marked "Hazardous Materials,"
Found in a Basement Storeroom
At The University of Chicago,
And Once Containing 64 Physics

physics physics physics physics physics physics physics physics

physics physics physics physics physics physics physics physics

physics physics physics physics physics physics physics physics

physics physics physics physics physics physics physics physics

physics physics physics physics physics physics physics physics

physics physics physics physics physics physics physics physics

physics physics physics physics physics physics physics   hxspics

physics physics physics physics physics physics   KABOOM   Pyhizs

physics physics physics physics physics physics   cinphs

                                                            piashy

                                                                 ysjphcs

                                                            spheyci

Brief Test in Physics: Found Poem with Prompt[a] and Radical Feminist Addendum[b]

"It behooves us always
to remember
that in physics
it has taken great men
to discover simple things:
the path of a stone,
the droop of a chain,
the tints of a bubble,
the shadows
in a cup."

—D'Arcy Thompson, *On Growth and Form*

[a] In four brief essays,
correctly attribute
each of the above "simple things"
to its discoverer,
then explain,
in layman's terms,
the physics
therein revealed.

[b] Look back at the language
in the previous items
and the substance
of the answers:
explain how clearly
physics is a patriarchal "priesthood"

from the inside out,
and thus is
"privileged."
Assess the outcome
of that privilege
in the extent of human sacrifice
orchestrated by those "priests."

"The Sky Is Falling. Do You Really Want to Be Writing?"

Nothing will come of nothing
—*King Lear*

Chicken Little is long gone,
her warning faded lower than world-drone,
cosmic idling of the Big Bang
parked like some dude's
getaway Cadillac
on the street out front
of the run-down apartment
where the universe will end.

There's a TV talking to itself
in the front room, and someone
might be in the
john, but nothing's
certain: atoms
smash into one another
inside our eyeballs
and we think
nothing of it,
even though
every afternoon, after lunch,
somewhere
in the hour of sleep
we need but never get,
at the tragic edges of the dream
we never finish,

three jagged bolts of lightning
thunder down beside us
and the person
we're talking to, that voice
in empty space,
doesn't even flinch.

Cosmology: The Word on the Street

At the very beginning Bossman light
the fuse: Big Bang. Shit flying everywhere,
planets, comets, meteors, little invisible
thingies, some with stingers and some with
bright hair and some that eat you alive,
make you skeleton in two minutes,
and then some that show you that skeleton
like a picture: X-Ray Man.

All this stuff making the whole whirl.
World I mean.

Then some other dude come in,
mess with it some more: attach names
to everything like
signs in the Five and Ten
25 cent everything in this bin:
quasar, galaxy, black hole.

Then about five thousand bazillion years later
and a whole mess of naked people
and war and like that,
we get here, man,
guns and crack and nightmoans,
and me with this no sleep hour
upstairs somewhere
in the whirl
and sometime along the night
we hear the phone ringing
but it ain't ours, we got no phone,

and after a time it drive us nuts:
Wo, somebody answer that phone

And somebody do, maybe even my own sister
who I ain't seen since fifteen years ago
maybe right across the street, there
in that apartment with the open window,
maybe my own sister answer the phone
and maybe me on the line saying
Is this you?
and she say
Yes it's me
and I say
Well this is me
and she say
Wo, Wo.

So where you go from there?
You got two doors and
if I see you,
you don't go through the one or the other,
but if I don't see you
you do.

See why I don't sleep?
Wakin up late
I start to think and thinkin
part of all the whirl:
heard one time wherever you go
you like to come back around:

whole whirl a circle,
some kind of tornado or swirly like a flushing toilet:

in the end it suck you and all you got right down,
house, shoes, girlfriend, light,
and nobody even hear you scream.

Big Bang come to that?
Bossman screw up good,
right from the beginning.

A Photo of Einstein in His Study

"In an experiment in Princeton, N.J., physicists sent a pulse of laser light through cesium vapor so quickly that it left the chamber before it had even finished entering."

— "Scientists Break Cosmic Speed Limit," Associated Press, July 20, 2000

1
Things, I see,
accumulate.
Having thrown nothing out for twenty years,
I spend three hours hunting up one poem,
written fifteen years ago
and never published: now it's
the very heart of something
I must finish.

Piles, avalanches, confusions of drafts and revisions.
All the hubbub in a stack of silent papers!

Time's arrow one way only?

How did this poem, fifteen years ago,
know this day—and book—was coming?

2
In the photo of Einstein
I come across in the pile,
he stands pensively, finger to his
bottom lip, head inclined slightly down
and to the right,

as if some problem
strange as Christ's nativity
were unfolding on the floor.

3
It is the moment
in which we all
are most human—
not Napoleon or Hitler or
even mad King Lear,
contending with the elements,
but the single person,
the forked, naked animal
isolated in a quiet moment
of primordial uncertainty,
the tiny present suddenly accumulating
dusty Chance and its flashy sidekick, Chaos,
new rules displacing ancient absolutes,
old meanings broken,
new disorders unfolding,
out of which breed,
no matter what we want,
Possibility—

triumph, guilt, grief,
Passover's blood on the lintel,
a cross splintered on a hill,
light outrunning itself,
Nagasaki sacked,
our past finished
almost before we've lived it.

The Poetry of Heat

A grand dream of physics is that if you heated the stuff up enough you
could not tell anything about it, other than its total mass, and we suspect
that at a high enough temperature, a pound of chair parts or of gold,
Gutenberg Bibles, or positron plasma would all turn out to be the same
thing.
—Wilczek and Levine, *Longing for the Harmonies*

We need to calm the language down.
—Robert Bly

1. Speed, Spin, Rising

I
I too would sometimes like to sit quietly
after the busyness of day.
Every evening, I would loosen my tie
and gather the ants at my feet.
"Make language," I would say,
and they would not.
"Do something," I would say,
and they would not.

But tonight I sit in the dark
and watch them lay down
their instinctive trails of fire:
a dance of circles under the hurrying moon.

II
I do not desire to loaf under trees
all my life,

or to spend time idly by the busy creeks.
I too want to wear the ten thousand leaves,
and to go the swift, intricate ways
over this planet of rocks.

III
Even the dead weedstalks are in motion.
The field has its galaxy of eyes.
Whirl is king.

IV
Consider the calmest birds.
They are made of fire, just like Butterfly Weed.
Inside them a hundred mayflies
spin in their cellular wings.
A thousand caterpillars
ignite their smoldering down.
A million grubworms
blaze up in their feathers,
learning to fly.

2. Photon Dance: Notes for a Noisy Summer Aubade

Rockspark, bunting feather, creekflash
fire the fox-quick dawn across Clear Fork
where sun comes swifter than word's waking:
rakelight strokes scintilla's mica-dance on air;
leaf-smear brightens from the muter blues downhollow;
in the deep of root-bank pools dace spin
bronze-watered shadows, silver-flecked and gold.

To hold these manifold commencements, spurts
and swaths of light, to catch day's bright composings

simultaneous as the sounds of weed-clashed, water-
raveled openings and closings, to catch world's chords
struck on wood's winds, on the scoured brass
and tympani of creeks
no one-word monotones will do: need color-scent
and eye-tune, counterpoint and symphony,

need tasting of the creeksheen glaze,
need hearing of the snail shell's inward flutings,
need touching of the bass-swirl under willowshade or snagfall—
need sense's fires transforming and connecting,
in the alchemy of sun and eye and water,
all colors, melodies, and textures:

then might come the song of cranefly,
waxwing, rockbass,
of snake-slick rock and quartz-scaled snake
whose blazed strains
almost stun
in this hot day's loud beginning.

3. Giftsong for the Rainditch

Toward spring meres
run the tricklets
where the wildbob thrums
and tumbles, where the slick-reed,
bright-tide sunlight
flecks the hurried green.
No death's breath hustles rustling
from this inch-deep: here breed
minworms, dirtstarts, hayspins.

And I am hale,
whole, and come hallowed
to this rainditch
where the mixing earth
and sun and waters
hotly swyve.

Blobs, Spots, Specks, Smudges, Cracks, Defects, Mistakes, Accidents, Exceptions, Irregularities

"...the windows to other worlds."
—Bob Miller, artist, quoted in K.C. Cole, *Sympathetic Vibrations*

1

      Regularly, Leonardo
stared at water-damaged walls,
         explosions, fires, battles, deluges,
eruptions, the manifold swirls of waters
     in fast rivers,
studied the blood-rich involutes,
        gnarls, folds, strings, clamps,
joints and messes of the body:
       all beautiful to him, as they should be—
alveolus, aureole, womb, gland, crump of anus,
      mushroom cap of penis,
folds and re-folds of vagina,
      dank sinusoidal caves,
complexities multitudinous as stars—
       all intricate, worthy of seeing, studying, drawing, and
         —blessedness!—
       all strange:

"You should look at certain walls
      stained with damp
        or at stones
    of uneven color,

                    the embers of fire,
                        or clouds
                        or mud.
            You will be able to see
                    in these
                    the likeness
                of divine landscapes,
        mountains, ruins, rocks, wood,
                    great plains,
                hills and valleys.

                    You will find
            most admirable ideas;
        from a confusion of shapes
                    the spirit is
                    quickened
                to new inventions."

2

    I study cloud chamber photographs:
            twenty horizontal tracks,
                    tightly packed, on plane, parallel,
            like a staff for music—
    particles close to the speed of light;
            then, superimposed,
                    two great clockwise spirals,
        and inside them, even smaller loopings,
            collisions, evolutions, devolutions,
        demolitions, then reconceptions
                of new veering, new vectors
        gathering motion and directions
                like life careening through itself,

forging heedlessly headlong
    then doubling back—
marriage, divorce, re-marriage,
    conception, gestation, nativity, death,

all gathered— all bunched,
              arrayed
in their reelings and unreelings
  then, even after all that,
      new tiny exploding clockspring
        spin-outs, their trails like writing in swift
looped words whose worlds I have yet to learn:

translated into other forms,
  the wild-determined whorls
of these particles
  are a troublesomeness of forces,
disturbances of many fields:
    locoweed in the bean patch,
      poison ivy rampant in the end zone,
        history complicated with mechanics,
          movement searching for a resting place despite momentum,
        perspective sweet-talked then seduced by calculus:
        tornadoes, Coriolus effects, hurricanoes,
    Bach's music broken, never coming back
      upon itself, dance
        lost off the edge of the stage,
tragedy incomplete, symphonies decayed to mere
          humming and droning,
      sudden clashes of cymbals,
        faint tinklings, triangular and glassy clatters,
        gear-chatters,
      escapement ticktock ratchetings—

>   tentative involvements of loosened strings
>   and idle dis-
>   solutions,

>   empty

>   winds

3

Yet, the map of one day's thoughts,
    orbiting around some as yet unseen notion,
takes me adventuring through blip and byte and fact
    towards something—what?—

                A.

            I breakfast on a page
        of numbers gathered by Annie Dillard,
            part of "The Wreck of Time,"
    and read where she discusses with her daughter
        six-figure deaths in a day, in stormflood, Bangladesh,
            thinks how difficult to visualize the bodies
                until her daughter says, thoughtful,
                    God-like down-looking playful and sad:

                "Lots   and   lots   of   dots,

                    in   blue   water."

                "Lightning strikes the planet
        about a hundred times each second,"
                    Dillard later writes: Oh yes.

"We arise from dirt and dwindle to dirt,
and the might of the universe is arrayed against us."

THUS

Blobs, blebs, spots, dots, specks, smudges, cracks,
defects, mistakes, accidents, exceptions, irregularities.

B.

Reading that same morning
Hopkins' "Wreck of The Deutschland,"
with its "brilliancy, starriness,
quain, its margaretting,"
its "freaks and graces"
and the inscaping, instressing
strange attracting of all things
"fickle, freckled, pied, couple-colored— who knows how,"
launched on mystery, chance, hap, my wild-determined course,

I am reminded of those dots on blue water,
of the might of the universe arrayed against us,
of the soft hands of drowning nuns,
of the might of waves, troughs and crests devouring,
of the rhythm and pitch of the poetry,
of the expanding and contracting tension of the lines,
of the wave-like alternations;
I am reminded that the might of the universe
is also arrrayed within us,
whole cosmoses of thought and feeling
as yet undiscovered, unnamed,
language-probes, word-shuttles within which to to explore

loomings large as Moby Dick,
knots as small as the Planck Time,
   riddles as strange as Schroedinger's Cat, the Violet Catastrophe,
    Szerpinski's Carpet,
whole jabberwockies of fact-imagined portmanteau quarky revelations:

        " Thus we can say
     that anything that develops
        in our universe,
     be it a young star in formation,
          plant life
     or the body of an animal,
         literally eats
     buzzing, blooming confusion—
        and in the course
     of doing so,
       breaks symmetry
     or becomes non-linear.
          In fact it is
     the break in symmetry
     (called a 'strange attractor')
   that triggers
         "chance variation"
             or development..."

             THUS

blobs, spots, quains, specks, smudges, cracks,
       defects, margarettings, freckleds, freakings, pieds,
          mistakes, accidents, exceptions, irregularities,
            thrawn, off-thrown misfit
    irregularities.

C.

Just after that I am attracted somehow,
   (by what miscellaneous notions?)
   (by what cosmic intentions?)
   (what random concatenations?)
  to Hardy's "The Convergence of the Twain"
with its "thrawn and throes,"
with its language struggling to sing and singing in struggle,
   its interconnectings and coincidences,
its synchronicities and blind happenstance and horror
    of the void occupied only by Dicing Time
and the piecemeal mess of Catastrophe and
  all falls and Falls,
  the ship's sinking in
"sparkles bleared and black and blind"

 and like a vessel vastly at sea,
  I am adrift myself, purposefully accidental,
expecting anything/nothing, meandering,
spinning, dancing, serendipitying
into this pool, this mere mirror, this ocean Titanic
and quickened by this confusion—
O most happy Latinate and portmanteau of words!—

    con fusion

of icebergian mindforms/ melting and reforming lifeshapes/
metamorphic bodies of thought/thoughtbodies/thoughtshapes

I myself sing myself, I myself sink myself,
to there mull pregnantly in amniotic depths
                unsuspected, unmapped:

                O Atlantis of discovery!
deep-dived toward in those five nuns' drowning!
        O sunken port of thought Titanic!
Sought out eighty years after accident
        addressed you, now telling
  your whole story for the first time—
O abyss blessedly alive with form—
        O smoking black vent of undersea mind
around which are arrayed and clear
        in unexpected light
life's eternal new inventions!
        O galactic womb-furnaces
where stars start in blue-red venous cloudiness!
        O Hubble of creation!
O seeing eye and mind!
                O world that wills sight
                then waits to be seen!

4

        Jackson Pollock,
alive with his wide brush,
                sloshing buckets of paint,
hunched before his canvas,
        ready to engage or channel the chaos,
climb aboard the speeding

whirl of things,
            cold-blooded and attentive
as a hunter even in
    the collected
                frenzy of his making,
even though
            as tightly wound as those
    decaying orbits
in the cloud chamber,
    he suddenly begins,
    loose, wild, smiling,
flinging uranium yellow
            across the upper quadrant
of the canvas, then blood
                scarlet across its center, then black,
spattered like
            Hiroshima's after-bomb-burst rain
across its length and breadth,

and the eye trembles and delights to see it,
            "the fascination of the abomination,"
                    this danse macabre with paint and color, spatter and dab,
        galliard of dribble, trickle, streak,
                resolving into nothing clearer than that
heaven-haven hell-hall
                    which is the swart blotched heart of things:

    all the violence of creation
    still vibrating everywhere,
background hiss of the Big Bang,
    that making of all vibration and locality:
of hummingbird and
            humming sweep of a billion galaxies' spiraling arms,

or click beetle and
    static's tick across space,
of pigment, canvas, and painter
    all brought trembling and resonant together
at the moment of creation,
    all the avalanche and momentum
                gathered in the gorgeous rockface of the mountain,
all the swirl and stomp and crushing and dismemberment
        collected and expressed in storm surf,
all the energy and horror of the imperial impulse,
        dizzying beautiful eddy of the Great Spot of Jupiter,
locust's blizzard of fecundity,
        fibrillation of the failing heart—

all leaping and jumping and involved in
    randomness, chaos,
      strangely attracting at last into
message and moment and meaning,
    and miracle!
    like church bells shaken in an earthquake,
Irish keening,
    Viking Berserkers screaming into battle,
moans of flushed lovers abed—
    like the last great chord
at the end of *Abbey Road,*
    that grating of the spheres
that turns us on

        then turns on us.

"These men who so extol
    incorruptibility,
      inalterability,

and so on,
speak thus,
I believe,
out of the great desire
they have
to live long
and for fear
of death."

5

Mitchell Feigenbaum, Father Chaos, observes the clouds:
trailing behind him the smoke of his cigarettes, he
uses up all his grant money on small-plane rides,
day after day soaring and circling among stratus and cumulus,
strato-cumulus, nimbocumulus, even the strange tornado-breeding
mammatocumuli, their weird lights, their bridges of purple lightning,
their pendulous dangers, their snakings down in tongues,
and before he can put it all in words, feels something there
of the truth, some similarity in shape, though in
different scale, some common edgy raggedness and wisping, some regular
tattering in wind, some distinctive bunching in upwelling globs of heat
from lake or field, some hydrodynamic and
aerodynamic mixtures and inter-involvings of clouds,
large and small—

clouds, their silken iterations,
their mossy recursiveness,
their sameness-within-scale
(one small part of a cloud is as foamy and

pouched and spongy as any whole
cloud—the same shape, really)
or to restate the (now) obvious:

> one local edge of cloud however
> shirred or puckered or hemmed
> is, he sees, like every edge of cloud
> everywhere—*e pluribus unum*,
> sameness in infinite
> (like snowflakes') variety

and clouds taking wind's shape
and temperature and the flow of
light and heat upwelling and
alpine, downwarding cold

> and who knows—in dream
> perhaps something of the shape
> of thought itself, that isolated-then-massing-
> togethering of things, that gravity that gathers
> confusion
> of shapes to new forms: Darwin's
> evolution out of disparate-seeming facts:
> finches' bills, fossil seashells in the
> mountains,
> shapes of butterflies' scales, or

to discover further "unity of form":
Leonardo's "Deluge" with many of the same
moves as his little drawing "Stars of Bethlehem"
and both of them matching, in their spin and whirl,

wildly elegant cloud chamber ghost dances,
   microcosmic pavanes and galliards...

      Let us linger: "Deluge" the end of time,
           world, the race of humans, landscape smeared,
            smudged, spun and twisted, broken,
         washed cataclysmically away: yet the same twist
            and swirl, mix and involution— eddying
              chaos, fertilizing new beginning—

    is the "Star of Bethlehem": cosmic prefiguration
  of the coming once again to world of order,
    form, and flower, earthed, moist, unfolding silently
  in meadow, connected to the cosmic,
    to fury of pressure, heat, fusion, fission,
    all the hymns of hydrogen

      we dance ourselves to and the music
      which Mitchell hears behind his small
      plane's drone as he turns and
        counter-turns among the clouds,
        squinting, studying,

  framing his hypothesis among shape-
shiftings, among turbulences rich and inscaping,
while seeing in both cloud's edge and whole clouds
something alike, something of the same order

  of things, some leaping
  and gathering and plunging together
in yonder cloud, at last, now duck's bill,
now pillow, now obelisk, now, he laughs and laughs
to see uncertainty cystallize into fact: now
  "very like a whale."

6

World comes into being
        materially, raw,
gods inventing themselves,
        inventing the very mothers
who will birth them,
        propagating out of the field they are
as light progagates
        out of the field that it is:

as the poem propagates
        out of the mess and spasm and germ of material and mind,
already disposed toward the poem,
        the Original dicovering Itself,
ever unfolding:

        O blobs which are universes blooming,
        O smudges through which we may see ourselves unfolding
into oneness and clarity like the leaves of maple tree,
        O specks which are ourselves microcosmic, intricate as all
matter and time wrapped livingly together,
        O cracks opening between our joints to let the star-making space
                flood in
and enlarge and renew us, O Deluge, O Star of Bethlehem,
        O humerus of the poem growing that is my arm,
        bless me with your hithering and thithering
        into form and life and history,
And, Gerard, Thomas, Annie, Jackson, Leonardo,
        Mitchell, all you Hundred Seers, see:
praise in practice, take up pen, word, brush,
        chisel, keyboard, body into dance,
shape your place

in the continual star-furnaced metaphor-forging
creation and annihilation, ride the sine wave
    of being and not being,
the freshening dip into matter
    and the ultimate mastering transformation of it,
extend toward always
    the momentous moments
to there where there is no between,
    where just *here is here*
in the stillness of your swirling flooded birthing lines,
    in the forever feverishly forevering
of your delicate dream-drawn down-looking
    dread delight.

Water into Fire

Despite the vision and the far-seeing wisdom of our wartime heads of state, the physicists felt a peculiarly intimate responsibility for suggesting, for supporting, and in the end, in large measure, for achieving the realization of atomic weapons. Nor can we forget that these weapons, as they were in fact used, dramatized so mercilessly the inhumanity and evil of modern war. In some sort of crude sense which no vulgarity, no humor, no overstatement can quite extinguish, the physicists have known sin, and this is a knowledge which they cannot lose.

—J. Robert Oppenheimer, "Physics in the Contemporary World"

To have built the bomb...was morally justifiable. But they did not just build the bomb. They enjoyed building it. They had the best time of their lives while building it. That, I believe, is what Oppy had in mind when he said they had sinned. And he was right.

—Freeman Dyson, *Disturbing the Universe*

[A wave] can separate itself from the original disturbance that created it and carry information far from its source, bending around corners, going right through things, sometimes capsizing people or even whole countries in the process. Once out on its own, its strength does not depend on any particular event or leader, but has a power that sometimes exceeds all expectations. It can interact with other waves in such ways that make it grow to monstrous proportions—or completely disappear.

—K.C. Cole, *Sympathetic Vibrations*

As a cloud dissolves and vanishes, so he who goes down to the nether world shall come up no more.

—Job 7: 9.

O head! Thou hast seen enough to split the planets.

—*Moby Dick*, "The Sphynx"

All of soul-inspiriting fled with sleep, and dark melancholy clouded every thought. The rain was pouring in torrents, and thick mists hid the summits of the mountains, so that I even saw not the faces of those mighty friends. Still I would penetrate their misty veil, and seek them in their cloudy retreats.

—Mary Shelley, *Frankenstein*

…in these resplendent Japanese seas the mariner encounters the direst of all storms… It will sometims burst from out that cloudless sky, like an exploding bomb upon a dazed and sleepy town."

—*Moby Dick*, "The Candles"

Can we ring the bells backward? Can we unlearn the arts that pretend to civilize, and then burn the world? There is a March of Science. But who shall beat the drum for its retreat?

—Charles Lamb, letter to George Dyer on the Lucifer Match, invented 1827

I knew a barber once who refused to give a discount to a bald client, explaining that his artistry consisted, not in the cutting off, but in the knowing when to stop.

—Wendell Berry, "Getting along with Nature"

Essay of the Body as Cloud Chamber

There's a divinity that shapes our ends,
Rough hew them how we will.
—*Hamlet* Act V

DANCING GRAINS

1827: Robert Brown
looks through his microscope:
pollen grains in water.
No matter what he does—
lifting his hands in the air,
balancing delicately, hands folded
firmly behind his back, even waiting for
the Cambridge carriages to pass outside
and so dampen all vibration—
no matter what, the grains dance,
jiggle, jump.

Brown thinks it
some manifestation
of the vital principle
in the pollen:
movement attends all life.
So he prepares another
viewing: dye particles,
certainly not living,
but they, too, "dance
the tarantella,"
the in-built reel and jig of things.

Where Aristophanes had said, "Whirl is king,"
Brown has no explanation.

Only much later
is it understood
that this dance in water
is "the first directly observed evidence"
of the atomic nature of all matter.

Brownian Motion:
molecules of transparent water, cloud-stuff,
made of unseen atoms,
push against the tiny pollen grains:
real things banging against
real things,

the invisible moving the visible:
Now you don't see it,
now you do.

***

O angels of sense, tell us:
how solid solid?
how gaseous gas?
Fogged in gray dawn,
half-awake in bed
after deepest sleep,
my flesh still delicate-seeming as mist,
I remember dreaming of St. Sebastian,
martyr, pierced by a thousand arrows,
eyes inclined unblinkingly heavenward,
as if beseeching the shafts of light

to increase their terrible
punctuation.

PARTICLES IN FLIGHT

1895: swathed in damp stratus and cumulus,
Charles Wilson
stands atop Ben Nevis, in Scotland,
the highest point in Great Britain,
admiring the clouds,
their lean sheeting and spiring,
their filmy clinging and parting,
their veil-like revealing and concealing—
all swirling like spirit
and shaping beauty out of air.
Later he tries in miniature
to create them
in his Cambridge lab:
not only beauty,
but for science.

Thus comes about
"the first detector to reveal
subatomic particles in flight,"
Wilson's cloud chamber,
small vault of delicacy,
its air pumped out,
and though successful,
bringing about condensation,
clouds' visibility out of
simple unseen vapor,

he finds even more
than his beloved mistings there:

Water droplets form
along the ionized paths
of the heretofore unseen:
ghost trails,
signatures of some unnamed presence,
fern-like curves of particles,
real things with charge
and velocity and mass,
and the world is there,
that common day, completely changed.

Years earlier, Luke Howard, after
studying London sky and weather,
publishes a book
first naming and classifying clouds—
nimbus, cirrus, stratus, cumulus—
and elicits from Goethe
these praising lines:

He grips what cannot be held, cannot be reached,
He is the first to hold it fast,
He gives precision to the imprecise, confines it,
Names it tellingly!—yours be the honor!—
Whenever a streak...climbs, piles itself together, scatters, falls,
May the world gratefully remember you.

—So too you, Wilson.
Cloudmaster, the unlucky.

***

It is not always what we want to see
that we see.
The child fallen from the railway overpass,
blood painting the constellations of disaster
on the pavement below,
the wrecked landscape after earthquake.

In Wilson's tight-built chamber
all the world grew larger, stranger,
more dread and alien in an instant,
one more knot of mystery unraveling into
tangled raptures of power—
power large as the flailing of galaxies' arms,
intense as the rush and punch of particles
through solid-seeming rock or
salt, or women, or seas, or gold—
sleeting of particles against particles so small,
and through interstices and spaces so
minute as not to be imagined,
but all astir and dancing,
shot through with photons and waves,
gamma particles and x-rays
like arrows of light—
martyr-matter,
the stuff of St. Sebastian.

And something else there
in Wilson's momentary clouds,
something like fire,
though larger and hotter,
more dread and unseen

than known before in nature
here below, or along the river Cam's
quiet fog,
or lonely dim Ben Nevis.

***

O body do not cease your common
plausibility even under pain,
lose not your functions and boundaries
to anger, grief, rage,
to the greed for knowledge that kills,
the easy shutters coming down over shame
and obligation,

but only give in to the inevitable infinite,
at the event horizon
of the Singularity
that will take you back,
compress you
into the single node of
possibility that you were
before your slow gestative explosion
into trunk and fingers and head and bowels,
rich and growing target for Time's arrow.

***

This noon, eating soup at the table,
I am drilled by a particle
from so far away

no number can name its distance,
its passage through me
almost as brief "as
the time it takes light
to travel
from one side of a proton
to the other."

What have I to do
with such incomprehensible intervals,
impossible divisions,
cosmic minuscules,
such grainy specks of world-stuff,
however much they maul
the nucleus of a cell,
set cancer starting,
or evolution on another tack,
ever unreeling its essays and revisions,
tirelessly scrawling them on
Time's bloody tables?

I think of Whitman's
noiseless patient spider,
"in measureless oceans of space,"
cosmic weaver of the strings and geodesics of creation,
launching forth "filament, filament, filament
out of itself,"
"ceaselessly musing, venturing, throwing,
seeking the spheres to connect them."

Out there, billion-eyed,
large as astronomy,
world-spider warps vast troughs and crests of space,

nets of attraction and momentum,
increasing always like some Titan
feeding blindly on what litter or life drifts by,
or is snared in its grave come-hithering:

and labors so, knitting and unknitting,
creating and destroying,
grumbling and transforming,
devouring, evacuating,
eating its own dung

per omnia saecula saeculorum

***

Professor Wilson, quiet in the Cambridge winter
with your microcosmic clouds,
gossamer-thin and silk-faint trails piercing them
then evanescing,
did you dream that day a world of
energy and dark-charmed strangeness?
Did you know that you, too,
were almost as airy as your beloved clouds,
certainly so pierced,
a thinking misty lattice of flesh and mind and soul,

quanta-bundles, local energy
moving causally through Time and Thomson's lab,
and could you, in that English cold December,
know or bear to know
Hiroshima or Nagasaki
in the heat of August
forty years away,

though already woven into you,
moving back through time
as electrons momentarily can do,
your life and work a new thing utterly,
uncontrollable,
not of your choosing, the future
in all its bifurcations and complexities
innominate, obtuse, incorrigible,
ever to grow more chaotic—
could you know the smallness of this Now,
your pretty
home-made clouds,
would lead to death and horror?

Could you have known, have traced
on the glass of your cloud chamber
the unfolding of this story,
packed like a nucleus
with particles and details
and unexpected energies:
a story in which yourself, a peaceable man,
devout, reverent,
meticulous,
and your cloudy
and buffeted Ben Nevis,
along with vacuums, atoms,
New Mexico, Japan,
poetry, Goethe,
water and fire,
would combine, there fuse and coalesce,
then burst forth,
out of their stormy accumulations,
iterations of time and chance and tragedy,

out of human spirit and mind set free,
the cloud that rose called Trinity?

SLOW NEUTRONS

1933: Gilbert Newton Lewis, chemist,
produces the first substantial quantity
of deuterium, known as "heavy water,"
first isolated by Harold Urey,
water with an isotope of hydrogen whose nucleus
carries a neutron.

Natural but rare.
Lewis works patiently to find
and concentrate it.

Its future use: to slow the neutrons
in atomic reactions,
to make possible the chain reaction:

possible the bomb.

FISSION

Early autumn, 1933.
London obscured by clouds
—the type Luke Howard
had classified as stratus—
accumulating, condensing:
occasional cold rain throughout that day.
Leo Szilard 35, expatriate,
social idealist, reformer,
friend of H.G. Wells who has just published

The Shape Of Things To Come,
Szilard, out walking nowhere in particular,
thinking about international affairs,
not much about physics,
suddenly has a flash:

nuclear fission,
the chain reaction, is possible.

It could save the world, he thinks.

Shadows in the shapes of clouds
float like old barrage balloons
across empty Russell Square.

***

Here in body, this world, this word, this scene,
this drama of forces and fictions,
the largest and the smallest
meet, interact,
are One, consciousness their field.
Thinking of the vastness
of the universe, I am simultaneously the site
of quantum exchanges, transformations:
language, chemistry, electricity, memory,
somehow giving over
into image.
I remember Menelaus
and the Old Man Of The Sea:
"He had his tricks, that god,
and would change into fire,
a tree in full leaf, a pride of savage lions,

into yourself, squalling as an infant.
But you had to hold on,
no matter how strange, how fearful, how
dangerous his shape:
truth only to those
who gripped his transformings tight."
And I think of Wilson's innocent clouds,
how they would have drifted softly through his fingers
even as he tried to grasp them,
tried to pull them back—
think how they swirled
gracefully, mixed and folded:
beautiful,
untouchable.

TRINITY

July 20, 1945, Almagordo, New Mexico.
Code name: the Trinity shot.
A star of green melted glass
on the desert floor
beneath its detonation;
a flash "that could have been seen
from another planet,"
Oppenheimer recalling Vishnu
The Destroyer saying,
having taken on his multiarmed form,

"Now I am become death,
the destroyer of worlds."

Isaac Rabi remembers watching in the desert:
"While this tremendous ball of flame

was there before us,
and we watched it,
and it rolled along,
it became in time
diffused with the clouds."

***

O body,
though I know
within us
all of creation's rush and hurry
is alive, Brownian Movement, gamma rays,
resonances with galaxies,
black holes, violent neutron stars,
all energy, evanescence, and power:
still, let me and those I love
"diffuse with the clouds,"
pass not torn or broken,
but solved like an equation
that comes out to zero,
subtracted from ourselves
painlessly,
all worked out.
Let us rest like Christ
between that death and rising,
dwell in motionless dark
wrapped in his cloudy shroud—
calm and lightless,
if only for the Planck Time
gone and still.

Always At My Back

"Time's winged chariot, hurrying near."

It arrives in no chariot, these days, but
rides elegantly some streamlined device
pulsed at near the speed of light
by its ion engine,
target lasered on my back
like the kill-spot of a high-tech hit man.

Yet somehow, I have stayed this long ahead,
though middle-aged and trick-kneed and tipsy,
wobbling through the eccentricities
of my life's decaying orbit
always closer to the insatiable
gravity of death.

So not mown down under hooves and wheels,
darkness all around, some soothsayer's bird-like cries,
crazy milling and tittering of the Fates
at the edge of the road,
but rather plunging silently into
extravagant and omnivorous light,
suddenly aflame and cindered
I will go, child of the time of Hiroshima,
child whom the hurry of the quantum
has entered and conquered,
and I will want not noise and lamentation,
grief, the violet catastrophes
of thought and memory undone,

but simply to return death to the earth,
to the human scale,
to the common moment in flesh.
Let me trail briefly across the upper atmosphere,
some momentary cloud
briefer than the flash in memory
that casts its ghost below
on a rampage of gas and heat;
let me seek a death
much smaller, more diminished by time
than those quarter million of fifty years ago,
smaller even than the high
glint of the approaching single bomber
or the shadow of an eyelash
just before it's smoke.

MY FATHER IN THE PHILIPPINES,
PREPARING FOR THE INVASION OF JAPAN

August 5, 1945, sunup.
In the mountains,
mist lying low in hollows between ridges,
clouds forming above, thermals
rising, my father, four years gone from home,
Hawaii, Guadalcanal, New Britain and
New Guinea, now the Philippines, Penay,
soon dispatched to Luzon,
wonders if he'll live.

This morning, all is quiet
save the dawn bird chorus
and the rising breeze that washes clouds
across the hills.

But last night, as in all nights, his dreams were
orange and loud: the *banzai*
attack came quick,
up out of darkness sudden faces
greasy with sweat and fear,
the buttons of the enemy's uniform
pressing in his face
as they wrestled,
clatter of Tommy-guns,
shrieking and yelling,
the sudden lucky punch of his bayonet
through ribs
and the strangely boyish weight of the enemy
now limp across him:
all this throws him face down from his tossing cot
into the bloody rankness of jungle,
choking on his fear.

So once more haggard, unrested at dawn,
he tries to calm himself,
remembers mom and dad,
his brothers Jack and Paul, the crazy dog
they once had that swam
beside them when they rowed the Ohio to fish
in West Virginia.
And he thinks again how the hills back home,
just across the river,
promised peace,
and how they make these same green slopes in light,
and how the mists and clouds like pillows
back there beckoned him

to lie down softly in his place
and drift carelessly to sleep.

PIKA DON

August 6, 1945: In hardly more
than the time it takes light
to travel across a proton
her skin was blistered and raised
by *pika*, the flash,
then flayed from her flesh
by the blast wave, *don*, which means "boom"—
all this in something unnameable as "instant."

Mute and deaf somnambulist,
she stumbled forward, one of several thousand
high school girls out that morning in the sun,
working in the city, now her hands held
out before her, gloves of her
own skin hanging from her wrists,
the shadow of her back
peeled and draped like
a blouse wrapped loosely around her waist:
like a cloud of skin
come loose from the sky of her self.

Many like her, in silent procession,
headed that morning to the seven boiling rivers
of Hiroshima,
seethes of black and red smoke
roiling above them,
lengthy cauldrons cooking blood and
ash and scintilla of children and factories and birds,

but found only corpses and the dying
clogging the banks,
those still surviving
unable to lower their ruined arms,
as if holding the ghosts of themselves
like partners in a dance.

Nor did the river stop the fires:
flames leaped them and
firestormed what was left,
cisterns filled with dead so tightly packed
they perished standing up,
roasted fathers the size of dogs
on ruined streets,
and then, later in the day,
a cold rain, black with soot,
brought from air
radiation's slow fire
into every wound and crevice,
burning rain, killing rain,
water transmuted into fire
in the alchemies of horror,
knowledge, fear, power, darkness, time.

"If only I had known,
I should have become a watchmaker,"

said Einstein,
near the end of his life.

The corpse lying on its back on the road had been killed immediately.... Its hand was lifted to the sky and the fingers were burning with blue flames.
—Hiroshima witness

Printed in the United States
1485300001B/571-588